CW01401523

better together*

* This book is best read together, grownup and kid.

akidsco.com

a kids book about

a kids book about

being in

foster care

by Seth Brauer

DK | Penguin Random House | **a**

A Kids Co.
Editor Emma Wolf
Designer Jelani Memory
Creative Director Rick DeLucco
Studio Manager Kenya Feldes
Sales Director Melanie Wilkins
Head of Books Jennifer Goldstein
CEO and Founder Jelani Memory

DK
Delhi Technical Team Bimlesh Tiwary Pushpak Tyagi, Rakesh Kumar
Senior Production Editor Jennifer Murray
Senior Production Controller Louise Minihane
Senior Acquisitions Editor Katy Flint
Acquisitions Project Editor Sara Forster
Managing Art Editor Vicky Short
Managing Director, Licensing Mark Searle

First American edition, 2025
Published in the United States by DK Publishing, 1745 Broadway, 20th Floor,
New York, NY 10019

First published in Great Britain in 2025 by
Dorling Kindersley Limited, 20 Vauxhall Bridge Road, London SW1V 2SA
A Penguin Random House Company

The authorised representative in the EEA is
Dorling Kindersley Verlag GmbH. Arnulfstr. 124, 80636 Munich, Germany

Copyright © 2025 Dorling Kindersley Limited
A Kids Book About, Kids Are Ready, and the colophon 'a' are trademarks of A Kids Book About, Inc.
10 9 8 7 6 5 4 3 2 1
001-349904-April/2025
All rights reserved.
No part of this publication may be reproduced, stored in or introduced into a retrieval system,
or transmitted, in any form, or by any means (electronic, mechanical, photocopying, recording,
or otherwise), without the prior written permission of the copyright owner.

A catalog record for this book is available from the Library of Congress.
A CIP catalogue record for this book is available from the British Library.
ISBN: 978-0-2417-4362-1

DK books are available at special discounts when purchased in bulk for sales
promotions, premiums, fund-raising, or education use. For details, contact:
DK Publishing Special Markets, 1745 Broadway, 20th Floor, New York, NY 10019
SpecialSales@dk.com

Printed and bound in China
www.dk.com
akidsco.com

MIX
Paper | Supporting
responsible forestry
FSC™ C018179

This book was made with Forest
Stewardship Council™ certified
paper – one small step in DK's
commitment to a sustainable future.
**Learn more at www.dk.com/uk/
information/sustainability**

To my birth mom, I will always love you.

To my siblings, I love you and I
am happy that you are in my life.

To my mom, I love our adventures together with
Sasco. I appreciate you for being kind to me
and supporting me on rainy and sunny days.

To Polly and Chelsie, thank you for always
being at my side when I was going
through tough stuff.

Intro
for grownups

When you hear the term "foster care," what do you think of? Whatever comes to mind, I encourage you to set it aside. Join us in this conversation from a place of curiosity and empathy.

The truth is, foster care is messy. There's a lot of hurt for families, especially kids, who are processing big emotions. It can be comforting to seek answers as a way to understand. However, the experience of foster care, for both kids and the grownups caring for them, is often characterized by uncertainty. There are no simple answers to questions that arise from these complex situations.

We invite you to lean in, listen, and learn. Kids going through challenging times have so much to offer the grownups in their lives. Creating the space for Seth as he wrote this book was humbling and expanded my perspective as a parent. Grownups, thanks for embarking on this journey with the kids in your life, and I hope that together, you'll discover new ways to support foster youth and families in your community!

Hi!

...Don't leave me hanging...

Hi!

OK, thanks!

My name is Seth.

May I share something with you?

Something that's a part
of me and **my story**?

Foster

care.

Have you heard of it?

Maybe you have,
or maybe not so much.

But it's OK either way because
I'm here to tell you **allIIIII** about it.

Foster care is when kids live with families who aren't their birth families.*

Sounds simple, right? But, there's more to it.

*A birth family is a person's biological parents and siblings—the family they're born into.

Being in foster care can be:

challenging,

frustrating,

confusing,

difficult,

and lonely.

Kids can be in **foster care** for a lot of reasons.

Sometimes for **days**.

Sometimes for **weeks**.

Sometimes for **months**.

Sometimes even for **years**.

I was **only 3** years old
when I entered foster care.

Can you remember what you
were doing when you were 3?

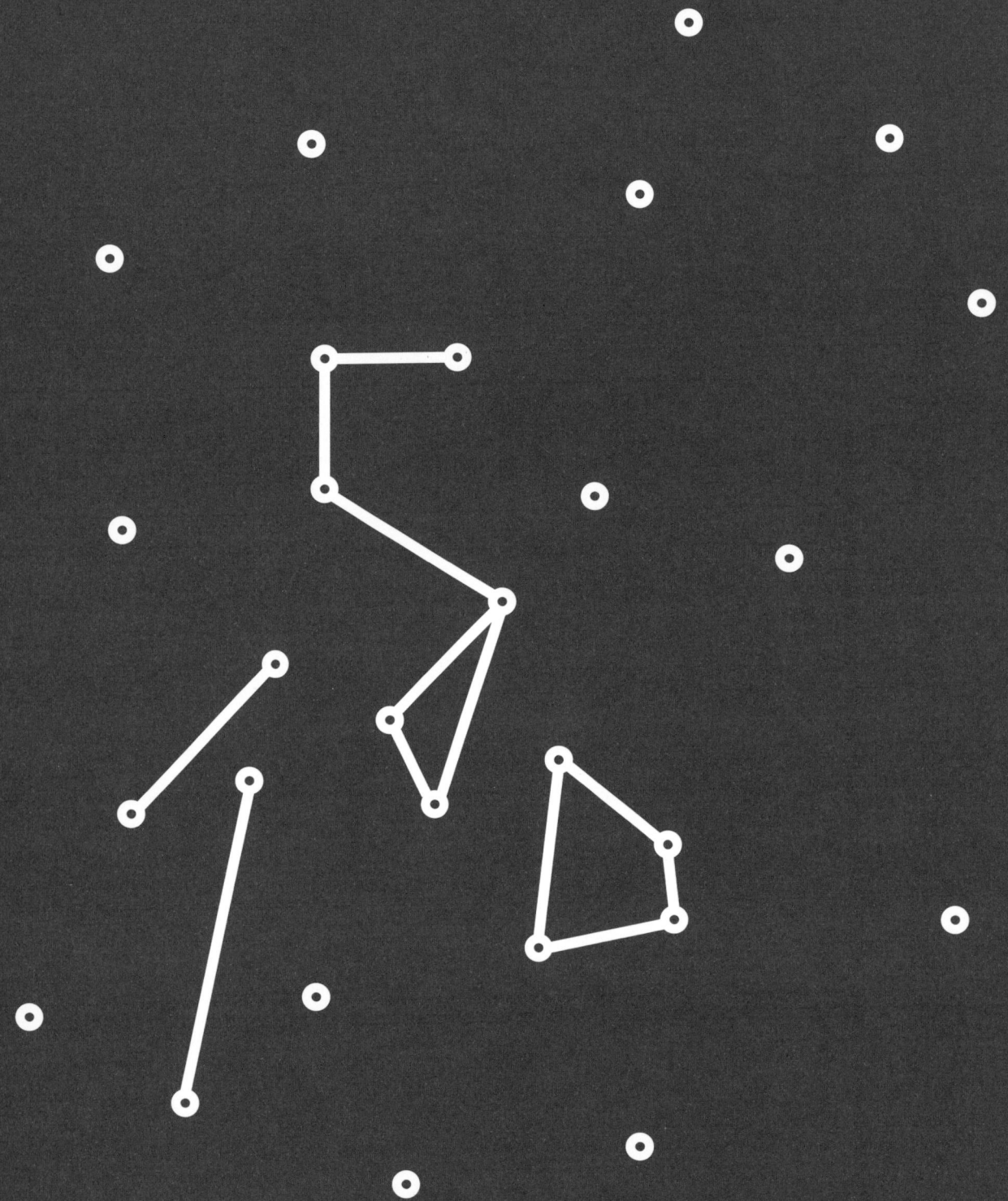

I don't remember everything.

But I remember **feeling lost**, and missing my siblings and parents.

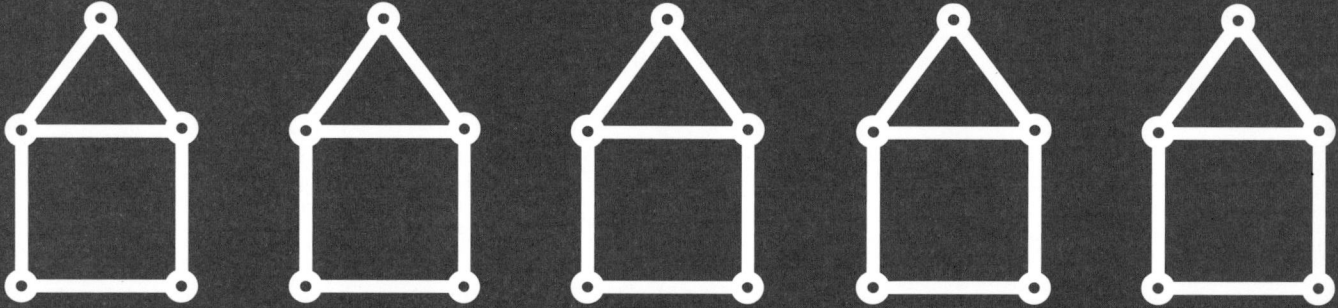

Imagine living in **10 different places**, from homes to hotels.

That's what I did.

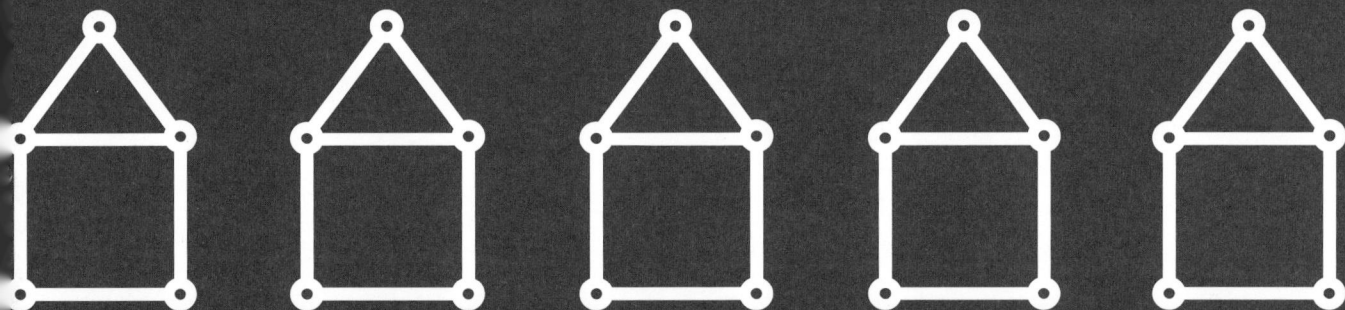

It was difficult to tell my story again and again to new grownups like social workers, counselors, and foster parents.

I was always meeting new people, eating new foods, and even going to new schools.

Every time I changed foster families, I had to leave behind toys, stuffed animals, pets, and people I really cared about.

Foster can whirl

care
be a
wind.

Sometimes people ask questions like:

"Why are you in foster care?"

"Are you sad?"

"Are those your real parents?"

Other times, they make guesses about me like:

"Your parents must not be good people."

"You're an only child."

"Your parents must not love you."

Ouch, right?

But here's the thing:

EVERY K[I]

EXPERIE[N]

FOSTER

DIFFERE[N]

D'S
NCE IN
CARE IS
NT AND
UNIQUE.

Like, did you know...

often, foster kids' biological parents love them a lot?

Or, that many foster kids are able to stay connected with their birth families?

And guess what?

WE'RE GO

OD KIDS!

Life in foster care taught me a lot.

Like...

You can't guess someone's life just by looking at them.

Kindness matters, especially to someone going through something difficult.

It's OK to feel big feelings.

Here's what my life looks like now.

I **play** sports. I love **soccer**!

I have a **dog**, Sasco, who I **snuggle** with.

I **walk** to school with my **friends**.

I don't have to move anymore, because now, I live with my **adoptive mom**.

I also have a **Gramma and Poppy** and a big family who I love very much.

I see my **birth family** sometimes. But it never feels like enough.

I miss my **siblings** all the time.

I've learned to keep my head up and be **flexible**.

BELIEVE IT OR NOT, FOSTER CARE TAUGHT ME RESILIENCE.

RESILIENCE means that you stick with

things even though they might be hard.

And I want you to know something.

Every p
you me
a speci

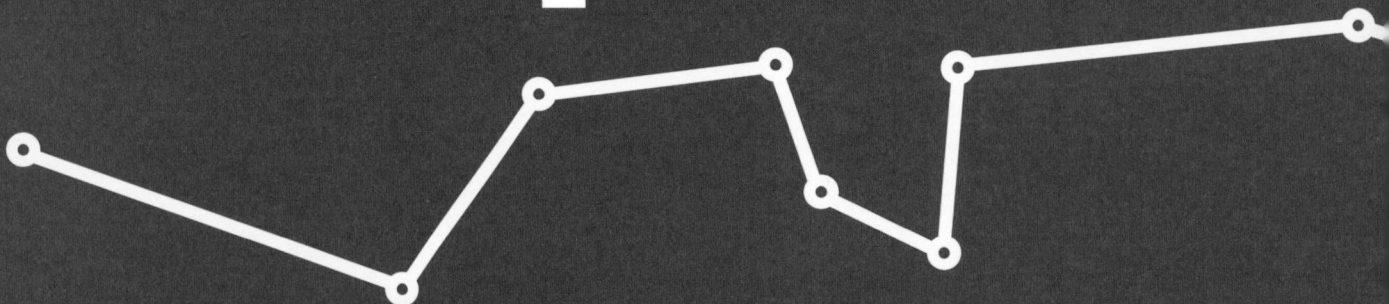

erson
et has
al story.

Some stories are **loud**,
and some are **quiet**.

Some are **happy**, and some
have **tough** parts, like mine.

Before you judge or guess,
take a moment to **learn**.

If you meet someone from or in foster care—or anyone, really—take a chance to **get to know them**.

Ask thoughtful questions and listen.

BECAUSE
KIDS,
LI

THEY'RE JUST KE YOU.

Kids who have feelings, dreams, likes, and dislikes.

EVERY

whether in foster care or not, deserves **understanding** and **friendship**.

KID,

And if you're in foster care,

KNOW YOU'RE ALONE.

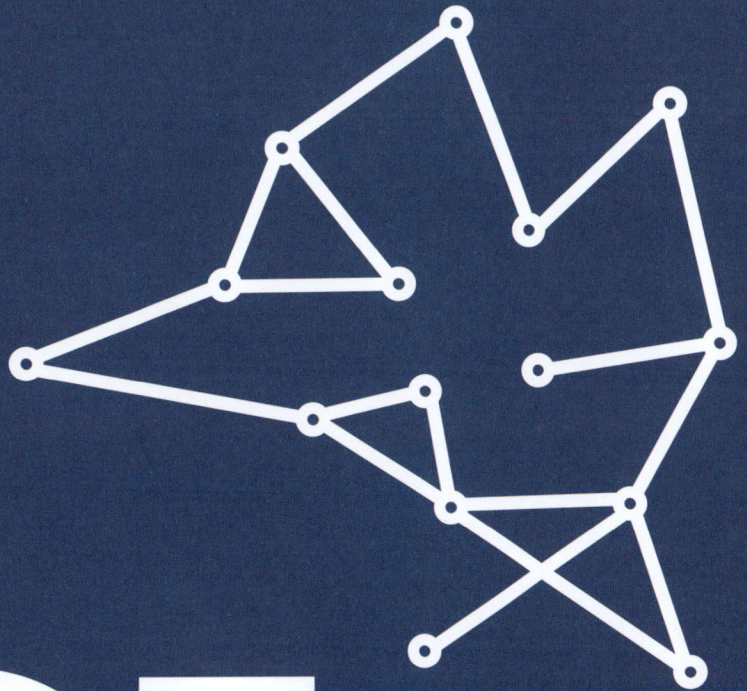

NOT

Every person's story has value.

Every story can teach, inspire,
or simply make us smile.

So, the next time you meet someone new, think of them like a book with a brand-new story...

just waiting to be read.

Outro
for grownups

We hope this book encourages you to find empathy for everyone involved in foster care—the experience can be overwhelming and uncomfortable. Embracing vulnerability goes a long way.

For kids experiencing foster care, finding stability can be challenging. Simply showing up and letting them know that wherever they're at is OK can help them feel seen. Let's focus our efforts on helping kids who may be going through a tough time know they aren't alone.

So, how do we do this? I'm glad you asked! The next time you see someone alone at school or having difficulty in the classroom, take a moment to say "hi" and get to know them. Grownups, take time with the kids in your life to brainstorm some thoughtful questions they could ask someone in foster care.

Remember that everyone's journey is unique, kids know their story best, and we can learn so much from listening. Stay curious!

About The Author

Seth Brauer (he/him) wrote this book for kids and grownups to better understand what it feels like to experience foster care. Having spent nearly 4 years in foster care, Seth knows firsthand how difficult it can be to process big feelings and answer challenging questions from others, and the power of friendship during tough times.

Now that he has had a chance to reflect on his experience, he's ready to share a bit about his journey. Seth wants kids who are experiencing foster care to know that they are not alone, and hopes that readers walk away with a sense of curiosity and understanding for kids in their community who may be going through a difficult time.

Seth's mom, Heather Ann Brauer, is a foster parent, an adoptive parent, and a coach—running and ultimate—who encourages kids to find their voice, choose joy, and celebrate little wins along the way. Together, Seth and Heather Ann are fierce advocates for empathetic listening, meeting people where they are at, and embracing vulnerability.

Made to empower.

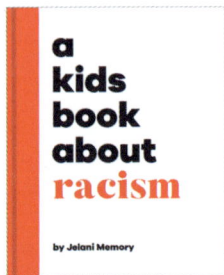

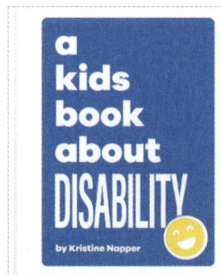

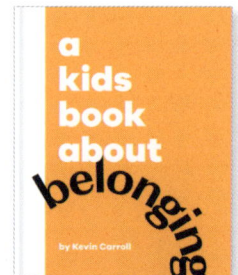

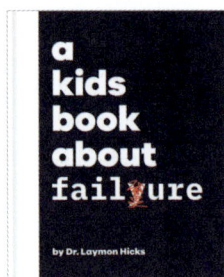

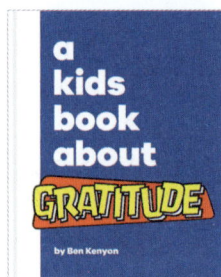

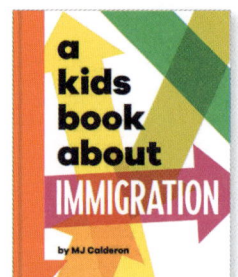

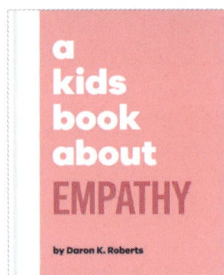

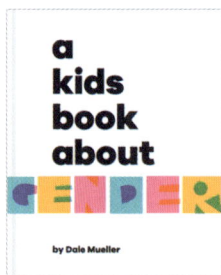

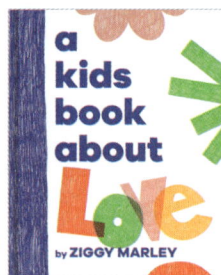

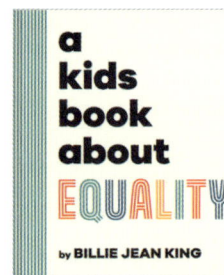

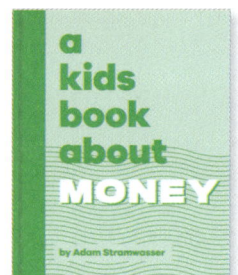

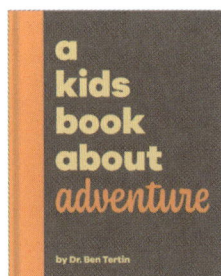

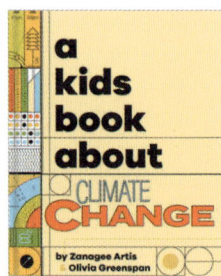

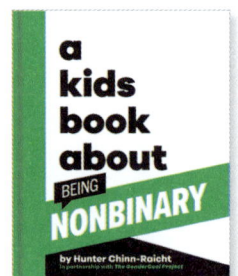

a kids book about **racism**
by Jelani Memory

a kids book about ANXIETY
by Ross Szabo

a kids book about DISABILITY
by Kristine Napper

a kids book about IMAGINATION
by LEVAR BURTON

a kids book about belonging
by Kevin Carroll

a kids book about failure
by Dr. Laymon Hicks

a kids book about GRATITUDE
by Ben Kenyon

a kids book about LIFE ONLINE
by Dave S. Anderson & Blake Fleischacker

a kids book about body image
by Rebecca Alexander

a kids book about IMMIGRATION
by MJ Calderon

a kids book about EMPATHY
by Daron K. Roberts

a kids book about GENDER
by Dale Mueller

a kids book about Love
by ZIGGY MARLEY

a kids book about EQUALITY
by BILLIE JEAN KING

a kids book about MONEY
by Adam Stramwasser

a kids book about FEMINISM
by Emma McIlroy

a kids book about adventure
by Dr. Ben Tertin

a kids book about CLIMATE CHANGE
by Zanagee Artis & Olivia Greenspan

a kids book about CONFIDENCE
by Joy Cho

a kids book about BEING NONBINARY
by Hunter Chinn-Raicht
in partnership with The GenderCool Project

Discover more at akidsco.com